Original title:
Enchanted Leaves

Copyright © 2025 Creative Arts Management OÜ
All rights reserved.

Author: Cassandra Whitaker
ISBN HARDBACK: 978-1-80567-022-3
ISBN PAPERBACK: 978-1-80567-102-2

The Language of Petals

In a garden where whispers roam,
Petals gossip about their home.
They laugh at the bees that bloom and buzz,
With silly dances, just because.

A sunflower winks, oh what a flirt,
Telling tall tales of roots and dirt.
While daisies giggle in fluffy ranks,
Dreaming of pranks on passive tanks.

Mosaic of Autumn's Heart

In a patchwork quilt of russet brown,
The leaves wear crowns like a silly clown.
Sprinkled with laughter from the sky,
As squirrels chat, both spry and spry.

Each gust of wind shakes a leaf's hand,
Wit as sharp as a captain's brand.
They tumble down like jolly fools,
Protesting the grip of nature's rules.

Tales Beneath the Verdant Sky

Under the trees, a comedy play,
Where branches sway in a funny way.
The grass rolls its eyes, can't take a joke,
As hedgehogs laugh, their spines bespoke.

A chubby gopher tells tales anew,
Of adventures that only the brave pursue.
While owls coo softly and try to see,
Who wins the crown of best in debris.

A Symphony of Green Veils

There's music in the rustle, a quirky beat,
As leaves sway along in their leafy feat.
Raccoons applaud with a cozy cheer,
For the band of trees that's quite sincere.

As twigs tap tap on the forest floor,
The fungus joins in, begging for more.
In this woodland concert, please don't miss,
The grand finale with a leaf-covered kiss.

Whispers of the Canopy

Up high the branches sway,
A squirrel's joke on display.
The wind carries giggles clear,
As trees share their gossip here.

Leaves wagging in playful jest,
Making nature's best-dressed fest.
Wonder if the owls will chime,
Or just hoot for a good time!

Secrets in the Breezes

The breeze winks and sways along,
Whispering a silly song.
Every branch a giggling muse,
In this colorful ruse.

A rabbit hops with a funny hat,
Conspiring with a well-dressed bat.
What secrets do the flowers keep?
A laugh bursts forth, it's hard to sleep!

Dances in the Dappled Light

Sunbeams play hide and seek,
While shadows stretch and peek.
A worm twirls in his leafy tie,
As crickets burst forth with a sigh.

In the shimmer, a frog leaps high,
Flipping like it's meant to fly.
All the creatures join the spree,
Nature's jesters, wild and free!

Chronicles of the Forest Floor

Among the roots, a tale unfolds,
Of acorns dressed in golden folds.
A fox tells stories with a grin,
While mushrooms giggle, their caps spin.

The beetles march, a funny band,
Playing tunes in this wonderland.
And if you listen, you might hear,
The sound of laughter dancing near!

The Dance of Twirling Fronds

In the forest, branches sway,
A caterpillar leads the way.
With moves so clumsy, small and sweet,
He stomps the ground with wiggly feet.

The ferns all giggle, shake in time,
A squirrel joins, he thinks it's sublime.
With acorn hats, they prance around,
It's a silly dance, no worries found.

Paths of Rustling Echoes

Oh, listen close, the leaves do chat,
They gossip tales of this and that.
One sighs, 'Did you hear Tom's new hat?'
While another mutters, 'What of the cat?'

The whispers drift like a playful breeze,
A tale of a frog who sneezed with ease.
They rave about foxes in bright red suits,
Dancing in circles with shiny boots.

Sighs of the Wandering Woods

In the woods where shadows play,
A chipmunk bursts forth, 'What a day!'
He trips on vines, oh what a scene,
And giggles out loud, 'I'm so routine!'

The trees chuckle, with trunk-like glee,
A raccoon laughs, 'Oh do follow me!'
With twirls and dips, they weave about,
A merry parade, no room for doubt.

Serendipity on a Gentle Breeze

The wind arrives on a kite-like quest,
It tickles the leaves, a feathered jest.
They twirl and spin, in playful cheer,
  While a lazy owl snoozes near.

It lifts the petals, high in the air,
A dandelion wishes it had flair.
It shouts, 'Catch me!' as it drifts away,
  The trees fall over, laughing all day.

Glow of the Woodland Realm

In the woods where critters dance,
The trees have hats, oh what a chance.
The squirrels throw nuts like confetti,
While mushrooms nod, all bright and petty.

Glow worms flash like disco lights,
While owls hoot jokes on starry nights.
The breeze plays tricks, it tickles and teases,
Making the branches sway like it pleases.

Secrets Wrapped in Color

The petals gossip, tales untold,
In shades of pink and marigold.
The daisies giggle, pat a bee,
While roses blush, 'Oh, look at me!'

The grass has secrets, whispers soft,
About the ants who clamber aloft.
But if you listen, don't betray,
A cricket might jump in to play.

The Alchemy of the Forest Floor

Mushrooms pop like silly hats,
Toadstools cheer, and so do bats.
The soil's rich like chocolate cake,
While rabbits sneak for an easy break.

The leaves are coins for fairy folk,
Some glitter, some shimmer, like a joke.
The foxes giggle, in clever plots,
Sipping dew from daisy pots.

The Soft Caress of Winding Vines

Vines twist and twirl, a playful dance,
Tickling branches in a leafy romance.
The bumblebees join with buzzing cheer,
While dandelions puff, spreading good cheer.

Woodpeckers tap on trees so grand,
Leaving notes for a woodland band.
The whispers of leaves, a chatty crowd,
Laughing so loud, they're feeling proud.

Swaying Silhouettes at Twilight

In the dusk, the branches dance,
With sneaky squirrels at a glance.
They twist and twirl, oh what a sight,
While crickets play their tunes at night.

The moon peeks in, a giggly friend,
And echoes of laughter seem to blend.
A shadow winks, a branch takes flight,
They tease the stars, such playful light.

Vows of the Vines

Two plants entwined beneath the sun,
Swearing to grow, to twist and run.
They joke and jive, a leafy spree,
"I'll hold you close, just don't hug me!"

With wobbly roots, they start to sway,
Making promises in a funny way.
Petals giggle, tendrils tease,
Together they cling, with such great ease.

Woodland Dreams in Amber Hues

In a grove where shadows lie,
A pinecone dreams, oh so spry.
He spins a tale of forest fun,
Of acorn races just begun.

The mushrooms chuckle, sharing glee,
As fireflies flash like VIPs.
A friendly bark, a splash of rain,
In this wild plot, no room for pain.

The Palette of Nature's Hand

In the garden, colors brawl,
The daisies giggle, bounce and sprawl.
Roses blush, a cheeky glance,
"Come smell my petals, let's take a chance!"

A dandelion's wish floats high,
"Pick me, pick me!" it starts to cry.
Each hue a shout, a colorful cheer,
In this vibrant party, we all appear.

Secrets of the Whispering Woods

In the woods, the trees all chatter,
They gossip 'bout the squirrel's new hat.
Branches shake with laughter and clatter,
As mushrooms giggle, 'What's up with that?'

A bird tweets jokes at the crow's expense,
Pine cones roll, trying to join the fun.
Even the old owl feels young and dense,
Flapping wings, he thinks he's number one.

When the Branches Speak

Branches lean in with silly tales,
Of sneaky ants and their tiny sails.
A raccoon claims he's the king of trails,
While acorns dance to their own gales.

Leaves tell stories in a rustled tone,
Of missed chances and silly blunders.
Each wind's whisper feels like homegrown,
Nature's comedy—a world of wonders.

The Radiance of Nature's Palette

Colors clash in a playful fight,
The yellow daisies poke fun at red.
Butterflies flit, feeling quite bright,
While bluebells giggle at what they've said.

A rainbow chuckles, drops all its hues,
As the sun shines down with a playful grin.
Even the clouds toss around their blues,
Nature joins in with a cheerful spin.

A Journey Through Verdant Hues

Let's skip through fields of silly greens,
Where snails wear hats and march in lines.
Frogs serenade with ridiculous scenes,
And grasshoppers boast of their best designs.

On trails where laughter spills and flows,
Awkward deer trip over their own four feet.
In the heart of the woods, merriment grows,
And every step is a silly beat.

The Magic Within the Green

In the garden where giggles grow,
A plant with a hat steals every show.
It sprouted a smile, quite wide and bright,
Dancing around in the morning light.

With whispers of jokes from the tips of the vines,
A cucumber chuckled, it's one of the signs.
The daisies all snicker, the tulips all tease,
As carrots wear trousers, oh how they'll please!

The sun sneezed loudly, the wind gave a grin,
The daisies all laughed, let the fun begin.
The leaves all shimmy, they wiggle and spin,
Creating a party, oh where to begin!

So step through the gate, come join in the cheer,
With flowers that giggle, and plants full of beer.
Nature's a jester, a grand, leafy clown,
In this whimsical world, let's turn it around!

Breathing Life into Nature's Tapestry

On a branch where the monkeys swing and sway,
A leaf wrote its memoirs in colors so gay.
It told of the breeze that tickled its skin,
And the chatter of squirrels, let the fun begin!

A rose wore a crown, quite regal and bright,
While daisies danced freely, just out of sight.
The oak told a story of roots intertwined,
In voices of Nature, both silly and kind.

The tulips tell fortunes, with pots full of gold,
As petals play poker, oh what tales unfold!
The world spins in laughter, on laughter we thrive,
While crickets are DJing, keeping the vibe.

So gather around, let the stories ignite,
With chirps and with chuckles, all day and all night.
In this canvas of joy, let your heart take a leap,
For the laughter of nature is ours for to keep!

The Magic Cradled in Green

In the forest, green things sway,
A leaf snickered, 'Come out to play!'
Squirrels dance with nuts in hand,
While mushrooms trip on fairy land.

The grass giggles, what a sight,
A worm wearing shoes, oh what a fright!
The sky blushes as the clouds tease,
With whispers of mischief in the breeze.

Whispers of the Forest Canopy

Up above, the branches sing,
While owls pull off an impersonating thing!
A raccoon wearing glasses reads,
The latest gossip among the trees.

Frogs leap high in purple hats,
Mapping out their comic spats.
The sun grins down with a wink,
As the petals giggle, don't you think?

Autumn's Secret Dance

Leaves twirl in their flashy gowns,
Donning colors that flip frowns.
A gust of wind, whoosh and glide,
The trees erupt in a leafy slide!

Squirrels take a spin, oh what fun,
Twirling 'round till the day is done.
With acorns flying left and right,
Nature's dance, a comical sight!

Lullabies of the Rustling Branches

At dusk, the branches weave a tale,
Of bashful beasts who dance and flail.
With branches bowing in laughter loud,
The woodlands sing to an invisible crowd.

The crickets join in, a band so bright,
While fireflies twinkle, what a sight!
A rhythm of rustles, a giggly sound,
In the forest's heart, joy is found.

Chronicles of Verdant Euphoria

In a glen where squirrels dance,
The trees wear hats, oh what a chance!
A rabbit with shades, quite a sight,
In this realm, everything feels right.

Bubbling brooks sing with glee,
Fish throwing parties, oh can't you see?
The ants have formed a marching band,
While butterflies take over the stand.

Mushrooms in tutus twirl with grace,
A raccoon tries to win the race.
Raccoons in capes laugh in delight,
This verdant world is pure delight.

So let us laugh as the leaves take flight,
In a fun parade from day to night.
Nature's humor, we can't outpace,
In this whimsical, leafy place.

The Substance of Shade and Light

Under canopies where giggles bloom,
Trees whisper secrets, dispelling gloom.
A fox in a fez critiques the chat,
While shadows play hide and seek with the cat.

Sunbeams tickle the forest floor,
As mushrooms giggle, wanting more.
A tortoise wearing a tiny tie,
Reminds us all to enjoy and not sigh.

Dancing ladybugs, a party of red,
While snails slide smoothly, never misled.
Raccoons with binoculars, spying around,
In this quirky place, humor abounds.

Hats adorned with flowers and dandelions,
Invite all creatures, no need for lions.
In the shade and light, joy fills the air,
Where laughter is found everywhere.

Echoes from the Sylvan Depths

In deep woods where shadows play,
Woodpeckers drum a funny ballet.
With a waltzing owl and a boogieing bat,
Who knew the forest was such a habitat?

Breezes tell jokes to the flowering bloom,
A chipmunk recites a poem in gloom.
The violets giggle, the daisies snort,
In this leafy comedy, laughter is sport.

A hedgehog tries on a pair of shoes,
While frogs debate which one to choose.
The ancient oaks roll their wise old eyes,
At the antics of creatures beneath the skies.

In the depths where echoes ring true,
Every twig holds a joke just for you.
Nature bursts forth with whimsical cheer,
In these sylvan depths, all laughter is dear.

Forest Stories in the Flicker of Light

With fireflies lighting up the gloom,
A squirrel recites from a leafy room.
Tales of acorns and berries so sweet,
While critters gather to tap their feet.

A wise old badger spins quite the yarn,
Of a dancing flower and its charm.
It tickled the bees, made the daisies grin,
A glorious tale of adventure to win.

In the flicker of light, shadows sway,
Wily foxes plot their next play.
A turtle laughs at the sprightly hare,
In this forest story, everyone's fair.

Cicadas join in with a rhythmic song,
In this playful forest, we all belong.
Gather 'round, dear friends, and share the delight,
In the magical moments of day and night.

Vows of the Whispering Wind

The wind made a promise, quite clear,
To tickle the branches, bring cheer.
Yet it tangled my hair in such knots,
I looked like a scarecrow—hardly a shot!

It laughed as it played with my hat,
Dodging my grasp, how rude is that?
A dance in the meadow with giggles around,
While I stumbled and tripped on the ground.

It swirled past the flowers, so sprightly and bold,
Claiming they were secrets, ages old.
But they're surely just gossip, or so it seems,
Falling like feathers from silly dreams!

With a flourish, it beckoned me dance,
But I tripped on a root—oh, what a chance!
I swore I'd outsmart this whimsical wind,
But laughed at my folly, where chaos begins.

The Lure of the Leafy Hollow

In a hollow of trees, so cozy and tight,
Squirrels threw acorns, oh what a sight!
They giggled and chattered, a raucous crew,
As I rolled down the hill—what a view!

A raccoon peeked out with a mask so sly,
Said, 'Join our party, oh me, oh my!'
With a snicker, I slipped on a mossy stone,
Landed on my back, not quite my throne!

The leaves murmured secrets, or so I believed,
While the otters laughed, 'You'll never be retrieved!'
I waved to the thistles, my new leafy friends,
Who promised to help me, but split in bends!

Then came the shadows, a wobbly dance,
The fireflies blinked, a mischievous glance.
The night whispered jokes, as I rolled with glee,
In this hollow of laughter, just nature and me.

Nature's Charmed Tapestry

The trees wore rich gowns of vibrant delight,
While critters performed in the soft golden light.
A rabbit in slippers, a frog in a tie,
Twirled across moss, oh my, oh my!

The stream called for songs of whimsical cheer,
While I joined the parade, with a giggle and cheer.
But tripped on a twig, went splashing about,
In a dance of the droplets, I laughed and I sprouted!

The sun beamed down with a warm, winking eye,
As I clambered on rocks, oh me, oh my!
A butterfly spotted, in a bowler hat grand,
Fluttered past me with a wave of its hand.

So join me for tea, said a wise wooden stump,
With mushrooms for cups, let's rise up and jump!
The tapestry woven in this playful scene,
Is laughter and folly where grace meets the green!

The Veil of Autumn's Gaze

Autumn peered through the branches, so sly,
With a wink and a nod, I felt it nearby.
Leaves tossed in laughter, like hats on the breeze,
Dancing down sidewalks, oh what a tease!

A squirrel in socks, wearing shades and a grin,
Challenged a crow, 'Come join in the spin!'
They twirled and they spun in a grand ballet,
While I watched in awe, wanting to play!

But I jumped 'too far' with a blunderous luck,
Landed in leaves, what a colorful muck!
Autumn just chuckled, with a rustly flair,
Said, 'Get up and laugh; embrace the fresh air!'

So I rolled with the leaves, what a silly sight,
Dipped in colors from morning till night.
For under the gaze of the trees' playful frown,
I realized I'm part of this whimsical town!

The Language of Dappled Light

Sunbeams giggle on the ground,
Whispering secrets all around.
Leaves play tag with shadows near,
Chasing laughs that we can hear.

Squirrels dance in leafy hats,
Making chatter just like bats.
A butterfly, with glee it flits,
Pirouetting in leafy skits.

Branches twist in silly bends,
Like a game where no one wins.
Dappled light and shadows tease,
Nature's humor, sure to please.

So join the fun beneath the trees,
And let your laughter ride the breeze.
For every leaf that whispers low,
Is a joke only the woods can know.

A Tapestry of Changing Colors

Crimson, gold, and pumpkin hues,
Dancing leaves, they tease and snooze.
With every gust, they spin and sway,
Laughing at us, come what may.

The trees are artists, bold and bright,
Painting scenes of sheer delight.
A rogue leaf shimmies to the ground,
In this carnival, fun's abound.

Pine cones giggle in their nests,
While acorns host dance-off quests.
Crows crack jokes from in the air,
While winds conspire with such flair.

So grab a leaf and let it spin,
Join the jests the woods begin.
For every shade that twirls around,
Is a punchline waiting to be found.

Shadows Beneath the Shade

Under branches, shadows play,
Making shapes like kids at play.
A cat might leap, a dog might chase,
While sunbeams tickle every face.

Funky shadows stretch and yawn,
Creating figures at the dawn.
A leaf reclines upon a stone,
While worms compose a tiny tone.

The grass is giggling, green and spry,
With sticky paint, it knows to try.
Dare to waltz with wandering vines,
Finding humor in sunlit signs.

So take a seat where shadows lay,
And let your cares just fade away.
For every glance beneath the trees,
Is a joke the shadows tease.

Petals of the Forgotten Breeze

Floats a petal, soft and rare,
In the breeze without a care.
It twirls and spins like a ballerina,
While giggling flowers join the scene-a.

Once a bloom, now tales it tells,
Of clever winds and funny spells.
A bumblebee takes break to sigh,
As petals whisper stories nigh.

The rustling grass joins in the fun,
Joking 'bout the lack of sun.
While clouds roll by, all fluffy and brief,
Cracking up like autumn's leaf.

So dance like petals in the air,
And let's be silly, free from care.
For every breeze that comes and goes,
Holds laughter in its secret blows.

Fluttering Silks in the Wind

A dance of gold and amber flies,
When breezes tickle, oh how they rise!
Turning circles, they start to twirl,
A leaf's mad journey, like a silly girl.

Silly shapes in playful spins,
Catch a ride on the breeze, oh, where do it begins?
They laugh aloud while teasing the trees,
In wacky games of hide and seize.

Whispers of laughter line the ground,
Poking fun at the squirrels all around.
"Oh look, there's a twirly spree!" they say,
As they flutter and flop in a bright ballet!

With a giggle, they fly so free,
Drifting down just to tease the bee.
"Catch us if you can," they call with cheer,
But you'll find them all giggling, my dear!

Portraits of the Shimmering Glade

In a gallery where no one cares,
Bright hues mingling, with funny airs.
A portrait here, a splash of sass,
Leaves poking heads out from a grassy mass.

With eyes so wide and grins so wide,
A critter poses, full of pride.
"Look at me, I'm a work of art!"
But a wobbly squirrel plays the part.

The trees lean close, they want to see,
What kind of masterpiece this could be.
"Oh, is that leaf got two left feet?"
No one can stroll like this on the street!

In the glade where laughter's spun,
A frame of fun beneath the sun.
Every branch is buzzing with cheer,
While nature stares, intrigued, my dear!

Whimsy of Nature's Tapestry

A quilt of colors, stitched so bright,
In wobbly patterns, a silly sight.
Leaves playing tricks, a charming spree,
Wrapping around my giggling knee.

"Boo!" says the red, "Peekaboo!" says the green,
While golden hues sneak in between.
Nature's jesters with ruffled flair,
Dancing around without a care.

Laughter woven, thread by thread,
In every twist, a chuckle spread.
Oh, the tales they could weave at night,
While spinning dreams in the moonlight.

With patterns quirking, crazy and bold,
Stories of mischief quietly told.
Nature cackles at its own sweet rhyme,
A tapestry laughing in joyful time!

Beneath the Canopy's Spell

Underneath the leafy show,
A wild mishap steals the glow.
"Watch your head, don't get conked!"
As a rogue acorn slyly plonks!

The branches chuckle, a jolly crew,
"Come join our game, we're playing, too!"
With swings and slides, the leaves take flight,
Whacking each other, what a sight!

While nature's laughter fills the air,
Silly critters bound without a care.
"Who knew splats fell from above?"
They squeak and tumble, all in love.

Cunning angles in a leafy green,
Crafting giggles, a leafy queen.
Oh, the charm of this leafy mess,
Dancing in chaos, nature's jest!

Shadows of Spring's Embrace

In the garden, laughter sways,
Dancing twigs in cheeky maze.
Frogs in hats, they leap and croak,
While butterflies play hide and stoke.

Squirrels gossip, tails held high,
While birds plot mischief in the sky.
Petals giggle, tickled by breeze,
As flowers trip on roots with ease.

Sunshine spills like honeyed wine,
And ants hold hands, a silly line.
Worms in bow ties, just a sight,
Spinning tales till the fall of night.

Every leaf, a dancer's dream,
In nature's waltz, they spin and beam.
For in this realm of joyful cheer,
Life's a jest, and all's sincere.

The Lure of Gilded Foliage

Vines in gold, the trees wear crowns,
Frivolous whispers all around.
Chipmunks host a fancy feast,
With mushrooms dressed as tiny beasts.

Acorns roll like bowling balls,
While raccoons run through leafy halls.
Every twig's a stage for play,
As critters dance the night away.

Mice in boots, they strut and prance,
While ladybugs hold a waltzing chance.
Breezes chuckle, leaves will tango,
Life's a party, just let it flow.

When shadows stretch and day goes dim,
The stars pour out like laughter's whim.
In gilded glades, joy never fades,
Nature's jest is serenely made.

Echoes Among the Boughs

Whispers echo through the trees,
Squirrels giggle with such ease.
Branches bend to hear the fun,
As shadows play, and day is done.

Breezes tease, and flowers laugh,
While woodpeckers sign autographs.
The toads recite their funny rhymes,
As sunbeams leap through tangled climes.

Chipmunks argue, who's the best,
In this leafy, leafy quest.
Every rustle has a jest,
In nature's riddle, we're all guests.

Amongst the boughs, pure joy resounds,
As laughter dances in the grounds.
With every leaf, a tale unspools,
In this verdant realm of playful fools.

Radiance of the Forgotten Grove

In a grove where shadows dwell,
Each crackling twig begins to yell.
The raccoons throw a lively ball,
While owls just chuckle, seeing all.

Mushrooms glow like disco lights,
While the breeze stirs sudden flights.
Deer in slippers glide on through,
As bats wear capes, quite out of view.

The branches sway, like silly dancers,
While rabbits cut through leafy lancers.
Every fern a jester's hat,
In this hidden nook, we all sat.

Radiance spills from every nook,
As laughter blooms, no need for a book.
In forgotten vignettes of wonder,
Nature's comedy and laughs asunder.

Nature's Celestial Dance

In the forest, trees sway, they prance,
Bending low in a whimsical dance.
Squirrels giggle in windy glee,
Shaking acorns like they're throwing a spree.

Sunbeams play tag, they bounce and dart,
Tickling shadows, oh what a part!
Leaves gossip in rustling tones,
Whispering secrets of silly old drones.

A raccoon beams with a crown of pine,
Claiming he's royalty, oh so fine.
A butterfly sneezes, the flowers all laugh,
As bees buzz around, taking a photograph.

Nature's own circus, a wild parade,
Where trees wear coats of the finest jade.
So come join the fun, it's a lively trance,
Where every leaf gets to twirl and dance.

When Woods Come Alive

At dusk the woods don their best attire,
Glow worms twinkle, lighting the spire.
A wise owl hoots with a touch of sass,
While a rabbit tries to impress in class.

From behind a bush, a fox strikes a pose,
Snapping a selfie as everyone knows.
Bears do the cha-cha, quite out of place,
Joining the critters in this wild race.

Mushrooms giggle, sprouting in rows,
While the breeze whispers jokes to the crows.
Each trunk and branch plays a silly role,
In this comedic play—their fun is the goal.

When night falls, oh what a scene,
Creatures all join, what a quirky routine!
Nature chuckles, its heart full of pride,
As laughter echoes, in this crazy ride.

The Cauldron of Colors

In the meadow, colors swirl and spin,
A rainbow argues, who's thicker—thin?
Buttercup grumbles, not yellow enough,
While violets whisper, 'Let's call it bluff.'

Crickets chirp in shades of teal,
Grasshoppers strut in a flashy reel.
The daisies mustered a vibrant debate,
While the weeds claim they'd make us late.

Pumpkin heads roll, causing a stir,
Saying they're the stars, in a loud slur.
Together they tumble, paint the ground,
A cacophony of hues, all around.

In this pot of paint, happiness brews,
As the colors giggle and trade their views.
Join the fun, in a riotous flair,
In nature's cauldron, find joy everywhere.

Enigma in the Evergreen

Whispers echo in the bristled green,
Where the secrets of squirrels can often be seen.
A mossy log swears it's a hidden throne,
While a chipmunk insists it's only his own.

Spruce trees chuckle, shaking with mirth,
Jealous of pines for their glittering worth.
A suave fox prances, tail like a plume,
Claiming he's the prince of this leafy room.

Under the canopy, shadows play tricks,
As rabbits hide behind stones made of bricks.
A woodpecker knocks in a code that's absurd,
For who else can understand this chirpy bird?

The mystery lingers, laughter draws near,
In this world where the weird feels clear.
So step right in, but try not to sneeze,
For in this green maze, you'll find a few leaves.

Kaleidoscope of the Wild

A squirrel named Fred wore a tutu,
He danced on the path, oh what a view!
With acorns as maracas, he'd shake with glee,
Even the owls blinked, "What a sight to see!"

The flowers were giggling, tickled by breeze,
While bees formed a band and played melodies.
The trees waved their branches, conducting the show,
As mushrooms in top hats began to grow!

A rabbit with glasses read jokes from a book,
The crowd roared with laughter; oh, what a nook!
Each critter held paws, a wild dance they kept,
In this vibrant forest, joyfulness leapt!

So if you're in nature, tune in to the fun,
You might find a party under the sun!
Just listen to whispers, the giggles, the plays,
In a world of wild wonders, let laughter amaze!

The Breath of Autumn's Symphony

There once was a crow who sang out of tune,
His friends in the trees chimed in quite a swoon.
With ruffled up feathers and a comical flair,
Each note turned the forest into a fair!

Leaves flipped like pancakes, swirling with grace,
While deer in afros smiled to the bass.
A turtle in shades called out, "Let's just groove!"
Nature's own party—how could they not move?

The squirrels built stages from branches and twigs,
While frogs donned top hats and danced silly jigs.
The wind played the lungs of this zany old show,
As nature erupted in laughter aglow!

So step into autumn and sway with delight,
Where every leaf quivers, and all feels just right.
The symphony of chuckles will wrap you about,
In this wacky wild kingdom, come join the shout!

Rooted in Wonder

In a garden that giggles, the roots start to chat,
About how to grow in their cozy habitat.
A carrot named Carl wore a hat made of dirt,
While the radishes laughed, calling, "That's how we flirt!"

The roses were whispering secrets of love,
As the daisies giggled, soaring high above.
A clever old worm with a monocle perched,
Declared, "Let's throw parties, we're all nicely birthed!"

The sprouts threw confetti from under the soil,
Inviting all bugs to their harvest-time toil.
They and the weeds had a game of charades,
While snails in tuxedos paraded through glades.

With chuckles in petals and roots making jokes,
The garden was bustling with giggles and pokes.
If you stop for a moment, you might find the groove,
In the realm of the roots, where laughter will move!

The Spell of the Silver Birch

A silver birch waved, with branches on high,
And told a few jokes that made laughter fly.
The critters all gathered beneath her green shade,
For punchlines and giggles that never would fade!

The hedgehogs wore capes, they took to the air,
While bunnies in costumes put on quite the flair.
An owl in a bowtie sat snug in the leaves,
Exchanged silly puns with the old rustling thieves.

These branches knew secrets of playful delight,
As dancing leaves twinkled in soft dappled light.
The forest would chuckle with every swift breeze,
While critters conspired in laughter and tease.

So come take a stroll by the silver birch tree,
Where joy's in abundance; it's where you should be!
Just linger a moment, let laughter unfurl,
In this whimsical haven, oh what a swirl!

Echoes of Nature's Hues

In springtime's grin, the flowers sway,
Bright colors shout, 'Come join our play!'
A squirrel, dressed in acorn chic,
Tries to dance, but takes a peak.

The sunlight beams, the shadows hide,
A rabbit hops, with silly pride.
Frogs croak tunes, a quirky band,
While ladybugs do fist bumps on demand.

Grasshoppers sing, a wild duet,
The fun won't end, at least not yet!
With nature's laughter all around,
It's a frolic fest, where joy is found.

So let's cheer for this leafy crew,
With silly tales that will ensue!
In this wacky, vibrant scene,
Nature's humor reigns as queen.

The Enchantment of the Twilight Grove

As dusk descends, the fireflies gleam,
They blink and wink—a glowing dream.
A raccoon steals from the picnic fold,
With snacks galore, brave and bold.

The owls hoot jokes, they're quite the hoot,
While bats do flips in a scuttling suit.
A fox with flair prances about,
As night unfolds and shadows sprout.

In laughter's glow, the breeze lets slip,
A gentle tease from a tree's wise grip.
Watch out for pranks by the playful wind,
As giggles rise where echoes blend.

So dance with glee through twilight's charm,
Embrace the quirks that nature farms.
It's a festive night, the fun's alive,
In this grove's giggling jive.

Mysteries Beneath the Turning Canopy

Under branches, secrets twirl,
Where squirrels plot their latest whirls.
A chipmunk's tale, it's full of zest,
Claiming he's the ultimate nest!

Leaves rustle softly, bringing gossip near,
A whispering breeze, 'Can you hear?'
The mushrooms giggle, quite absurd,
As toads debate, which hat's preferred.

A curious crow, with feathers sleek,
Mocks the wisdom of the meek.
Roots play tricks, tying up feet,
As nature's riddle is bittersweet.

In these mysteries, laughter swells,
With every tale that nature tells.
So wander deep, embrace the tease,
Of secrets tucked in playful trees.

Flutters of the Serene Silence

In stillness, wings begin to flap,
Butterflies dance with a happy clap.
A bumblebee hums a tune so fine,
While flowers giggle at the sunshine wine.

A turtle dreams, oh what a show,
With a sleepy yawn, too slow to go.
While crickets chirp, the gossip flies,
In a cozy nook, under wide blue skies.

A snail's sneaky race, oh such a sight,
He's the champ of slow, yet feels so bright.
And the pond reflects a glittery grin,
Where frogs leap high, sensing the win.

So pause a moment, breathe it in,
The quiet jokes that nature spins.
In peaceful giggles, take your chance,
To join the foliage in joyful dance.

The Caress of the Season's Breath

When autumn arrives with a chuckle,
The branches shake like they're in a shuffle.
Fallen nuggets dance with the breeze,
Crispy whispers, oh what a tease!

Squirrels joke as they gather their stash,
While acorns tumble with a playful crash.
The trees chuckle, their faces aglow,
As the wind's tickle becomes quite the show!

Joyful rustles echo through the air,
Leaves spin like dancers, twirling without care.
They laugh aloud in hues of gold,
Tales of mischief in shades so bold!

So join their jests, don't be afraid,
In this whimsical dance, let dreams cascade.
For nature's humor knows no bounds,
In every corner, laughter resounds!

Embrace of the Glorious Thicket

In shady corners, where sunlight peeks,
The foliage giggles and somehow speaks.
With every poke from a curious breeze,
Branches sway like they're ready to tease!

The bushes murmur with gossipy cheer,
As critters dart swiftly, chomp in good cheer.
Rabbits hop lightly, in a comical chase,
While roses lean in, to set the pace!

A chorus of petals, pink and bright,
Tells jokes to the stars, twinkling at night.
"Good luck," they laugh, "That one's pretty bold!"
In this deep thicket, fun never gets old!

So tiptoe softly, join this grand play,
In the arms of the wild, let laughter stay.
For here amidst greenery, absurdities bloom,
In the embrace of the wild, there's always room!

Whispers of the Green Heart

A breezy giggle flutters so near,
As leaves tell tales we long to hear.
With every sigh, and every rustle,
The forest chuckles, oh, what a bustle!

"Did you hear?" whispers old oaks wise,
"Last summer's gossip has turned to sighs."
Young saplings snicker, their branches like arms,
Swishing and swaying with playful charms!

Mushrooms nod, in their polka-dot hats,
While hedgehogs wheel, oh, how they dance!
Nature's festival, a comedic spree,
Amidst the greens, come join the glee!

So lend an ear to this green heart's song,
Laughter flows freely; it's where we belong.
In whispers sweet, and giggles bright,
Find joy in the woodlands, pure delight!

A Chorus of Twirling Leaves

Twisting and turning in a wild ballet,
Leaves leap and spin, what a funny display!
One takes a tumble, with style in its fall,
"Did you see that?!" they chirp, "What a sprawl!"

Like clowns at a party, they jig and they jive,
Spiraling down, feeling so alive.
The wind plays conductor, with a mischievous grin,
As nature's orchestra begins to spin!

From trees high above, they giggle and glide,
Scattering chuckles, in unison they bide.
Their colors burst forth, a sight to behold,
In a raucous display of laughter so bold!

So grab a friend, let's join the spree,
In this leafy chorus, so carefree.
Dance with the breezes, let laughter spill,
In a swirling cascade, we've found our thrill!

Secrets Hidden in the Thicket

In the thicket where secrets play,
Wild squirrels plot in a cheeky way.
They're stockpiling acorns, oh what a mess!
While birds gossip about the dress!

A rabbit's wiggle gives away a trail,
As snickering raccoons tell each tale.
The fox rolls his eyes, so quite amused,
At all the creatures that he's confused.

Trees giggle softly with rustling leaves,
As shadows dance, the sunlight weaves.
A chipmunk juggles, a funny sight,
As the woodland revels till the night!

From beneath a bush, a gnome peeks out,
With twinkling eyes, he gives a shout.
In this secret spot, laughter reigns,
Where even the fungi share their gains!

A Dance of Shadows and Light

A wobbly brook hums a silly tune,
While fireflies jiggle beneath the moon.
The shadows twirl, a playful ballet,
As critters join in, come what may!

A bear tries salsa, stubbing his toes,
While hedgehogs conga, lined up in rows.
In this wild jamboree, laughter erupts,
As the owl shakes his head and abruptly hops!

Sunbeams flicker like stars in disguise,
While rabbits perform their tap dance surprise.
A turtle wiggles, though moving is slow,
But in this crazy dance, he steals the show!

With giggles and glimmers, the forest roars,
As woodland friends bust down all doors.
Convert your worries to a jiggle tonight,
For shadows and light, they both feel just right!

The Forest's Lullaby

When twilight comes with a yawning sigh,
The creatures settle, the stars float by.
A sleepy raccoon hums a soft song,
While critters sway, where they all belong.

The trees croon sweetly, with whispers so clear,
As frogs in the pond croak out their cheer.
An owl nods off, but wakes with a snort,
As crickets compose a dreamy report!

A band of mice with fiddles they play,
To soothe the forest at the end of the day.
They prance through the shadows, they chuckle and cheer,

With each gentle note that all creatures hear.

The moon winks down, a chuckle in light,
As the forest cozies up, ready for night.
With each gentle sigh, dreams fill the air,
In this lullaby land, without a care!

When Colors Fade into Dreams

As day bids farewell, hues start to blend,
In a ruckus of colors that twist and bend.
The sun trips over, laughing in glee,
While shadows stretch out, as far as can be!

A green tree giggles, "I'm feeling quite blue!"
While daisies debate if they're yellow or new.
The blushing sunset is quite a delight,
As the colors all tango, through fading light!

The grass whispers secrets, a tale full of cheer,
While fireflies flash as if they're in gear.
With a flick and a flit, they invite all to play,
In this whirlwind of dreams, they dance and sway!

So when colors fade, it's not time for gloom,
Just a playful wink from the stars, in bloom.
As the evening giggles, a world now aglow,
In the dreamland of jesters, we all steal the show!

Captured by Nature's Embrace

I tripped on a root, it winked at me,
The funniest prank from the old oak tree.
With acorns launching like tiny bombs,
Squirrels giggle, in their fluffy floms.

The daisies chuckle, oh what a scene,
Their petals swaying, like a cartoon dream.
Nature's big hug, a ticklish surprise,
With buzzing bees that wear funny ties.

The Palette of Sentient Silhouettes

Colors dance, a raucous delight,
The sun spills paint, oh what a sight!
Red leaves tease the green with a grin,
While wind chimes laugh, inviting in.

The shadows plot, behind the tree,
Laughing quietly, just you and me.
They stretch and yawn, in comical poses,
Waving hello, with trembling roses.

Shades of Serenity in the Sunlight

A butterfly slips on a sunny sock,
Mismatched patterns that really rock.
The blooms giggle with fragrance sweet,
As a bumblebee taps its tiny feet.

Clouds play peek-a-boo, so absurd,
Throwing their fluff where laughter stirred.
Sunbeams bounce like a playful pup,
Catching silly moments, they never give up.

Dances of Light and Shadow

The fireflies flash, a disco ball,
Lighting up the night, with a ghostly call.
The trees sway wildly, in a dance so bold,
While the mossy floor giggles, stories told.

As moonlight twirls, it drags the stars,
Into a conga line, oh how bizarre!
Each step a chuckle, each twirl a cheer,
Creating a party that lasts all year!

Canopies of Captivating Calm

In a forest where squirrels jest,
The trees wear hats, a quirky fest.
Branches tickle clouded brows,
While fungi dance, adorned like cows.

The ladybugs form a marching band,
With tiny drums in heaps of sand.
They giggle as the grasshoppers leap,
In rhythm with the ants that creep.

Mossy cushions, soft and round,
Invite the gnomes to sit around.
And when the wind begins to blow,
The leaves do flips; oh what a show!

So wander in this jolly grove,
Where every twig has tales to prove.
A place where laughter fills the air,
In nature's light, without a care.

A Garden of Whispered Secrets

In a garden where the daisies plot,
The roses gossip, oh what a lot!
With petals ripe for tales so bold,
While the tulips spin yarns of old.

The carrots wear shades to block the sun,
As radishes giggle, oh what fun!
Pumpkins whisper in deep hushed tones,
While cabbage laughs with leafy groans.

A bug parade marches, oh so grand,
Each one strutting, a funky band.
With beetles breaking out in style,
While caterpillars dance a while.

So come and sniff the blooms' delight,
Where humor blooms, and life feels right.
In this patch where laughter weaves,
A song of joy among the leaves.

Guardians of the Verdant Realm

In the realm where the bushes speak,
The foxes play hide and seek.
Mossy knights clad in leafy green,
Guard the tales we've never seen.

With acorns dropping like heavy pearls,
And beetles racing in silly twirls,
The wise old owl cracks a joke,
As the wisecracking rabbits soak.

Dancing sprites in twinkling light,
Make daydreams leap into the night.
The mushrooms chuckle as frogs sing,
While swaying with the beats of spring.

So tiptoe through this jolly glade,
Where laughter's woven, never fade.
Nature's jesters, a merry scheme,
Invite you in to share the dream.

Colors of a Sunlit Reverie

In a patchwork world of vibrant shades,
The daisies wear stripes, nature's parades.
Sunflowers giggle, swaying high,
While butterflies flutter, oh my, oh my!

Rainbow-colored ants march in line,
With candy canes, they dash and dine.
The grass chuckles under our feet,
As we dance to its playful beat.

Clouds burst into laughter, fluffy and white,
While butterflies glide in whimsical flight.
A painter's palette spills on the ground,
In this joyous riot, fun can be found.

So jump and twirl in this lively space,
Where colors and humor reside in grace.
A tapestry of joy, nature's decree,
In a sunlit reverie, wild and free.

www.ingramcontent.com/pod-product-compliance
Lightning Source LLC
Chambersburg PA
CBHW072138200426
43209CB00050B/122